TURN YOUR COTTAGE INTO MONEY

How to rent your cottage and make
a profit in Ontario and Quebec!

by Tina Lalonde

DEDICATION

I would like to say thank you from the bottom of my heart. If it weren't for these people, this book would not have made it to publishing. *Lucille*, my banker, for making my dream come true by helping get the loan to buy my cottage. *Katrina*, my dear friend and detail person, for helping me sort out all the ideas in my head to make sense on paper and making sure I stop putting smiley faces... :-) Sorry, couldn't help myself. *Carol* my good friend, *Mike* my brother and *Serge* my true love for helping with renovating the cottage to make it more appealing, and teaching me that owning property is a lot of work. *Peter*, my cottage neighbour, for helping me learn what to do when things break down and to NOT panic, and just turn things off. And last but not least, *Tami* for the wonderful book cover idea and *Chantal* for helping me format the book cover. I am truly grateful for all the help and support you have all provided to make this book a reality and make my dream of getting my book published a success. Thank you from the bottom of my heart.

Yours truly,

Tina Lalonde

Table of Contents

2

Why I Wrote This Book

I bought my dream cottage, or what I hope it will become someday, but for now it is an investment and a place for me to enjoy getting away from the city. When I was younger, we would go up to my aunt's house that felt like a cottage. I loved it there and remember saying to my aunt that one day I would like to own a house or cottage and voilà…my dream came true. After 2 years of searching, I bought my cottage. My intention was to use the cottage with family and friends, but also rent it out to pay for some upgrades and pay for the monthly expenses, which it did.

Have you ever tried to find information, only to be searching everywhere and not finding what you need? Or maybe you found someone to give you some information only to be transferred to another person who eventually transferred you back to the original person? Well, that was me. I was that person who wanted to rent out her cottage as a business, but had to look everywhere for information and it was frustrating. It took me months to find information on what I needed to do to get my cottage ready to rent.

I wrote this book because I made quite a few mistakes that cost me both emotionally and financially. I thought, if I was struggling with this, maybe there are other owners feeling the same frustration. I don't want others to go through what I did and if I can help one person, then my struggles were worth it.

Maybe you have the same dream of buying a cottage or having an investment property. Whatever the reason, there are things you need to know about before you plan to rent out your cottage.

I wish I would have had this information before I started. I would have avoided many mistakes. Hopefully the information will be helpful to you or someone you know.

Good luck and have fun.

Tina Lalonde

Who Should Read This Book

You've purchased a cottage with the intention of enjoying it with friends and family, or maybe as an investment. If you are thinking about renting your cottage, which I believe you are because you've purchased my book, there are things you need to know and do before jumping into the rental market. This book is aimed at people who own a cottage or chalet in Ontario and Quebec and want to rent it out, but don't know what they need to do and what the rules or laws are for renting the property. In the following pages, you will learn about what is needed to rent your cottage, everything from setting your rates, finding renters, advertising to the right people, to completing your taxes. All in one location!

There is so much good information that I want to share with you, but if I added everything to this book it would look like an encyclopedia. I put everything you need to get started renting your cottage right away. Everything else that relates to renting your cottage such as government regulations that change will be added to my website, as well as new tips that help attract new renters and keep the old ones coming back. Go to my website at www.howtorentmycottage.ca.

Lets get started.

Chapter 1
What are your goals?

So you bought the cottage you've been dreaming about and are ready to start renting it out. OK maybe it's not perfect. It needs a bit of love before you rent it out. Really? Does it? It's not like you're renting a 5 star chalet, but maybe that is your goal to make it a 5 star chalet. The first thing you need to do is identify what are your goals for renting the cottage. Are they short or long term goals? How will you know you've reached your goal? From there, you will need a plan or strategy to reach your goal. This chapter will discuss what is a goal, the types of short and long-term goals, a business plan and do you need one, and what you need to reach your goal.

Goals - What are they?

A goal is a target of what you want to achieve and the length of time it will take you to get it. Are your goals short or long term?

What is a short and long term goal?
Short-term goal is usually a time frame ranging from 3 months up to 5 years, usually with a budget of less than $5,000. A long-term goal is greater than 5 years and has a budget greater than $10,000.

Here are a few example questions to help you define your short and long term goals:

- What are my short-term goals (within 5 years) i.e. pay the bills, winterize the cottage, or maybe buy toys for the cottage?
- What are my long-term goals (5+ years) i.e. pay off the

mortgage, or maybe move there for retirement?

- If I'm going to renovate, what will it cost me to upgrade the cottage?
- What do the expenses currently cost monthly and yearly? How much will the bills increase with renters?
- Are you going to rent it as a 3- or 4-season? 4 being winterized. Maybe 3-season may be the only current option, but you could add winterizing the cottage as part of your short-term goal?
- How often are you going to rent it i.e. daily, weekly, summer, winter?
- What days will you be using the cottage for personal use and not renting it?

Business Plan and Do I Need One?

The Canada Business Network describes a business plan as:

A business plan is a written document that describes your business, its objectives and strategies, the market you are targeting and the financial forecast for your business. It will assist in setting realistic and timely goals, help secure external funding, help measure your success, clarify operational requirements and establish reasonable financial forecasts. Preparing your plan will help you focus on how your new business will need to operate to give it the best chance for success (**Canada Business Network, Government Services for Entrepreneurs** (Date modified: 2012-09-17). Business planning-FAQs. Web. Retrieved from www.canadabusiness.ca/eng/page/2751).

Do you need an official business plan to rent your cottage?

Not unless you're planning to try to get financing or investors. A plan will help you set a goal, identify a target date and determine what action steps are needed to make sure you reach your goal. Once you've identified your goals, now we need to figure out what you need to do to reach those goals.

Have a plan before you start renting!

On the next page there's a mind map or a visual breakdown of what you should consider when renting your cottage. A mind map is a brainstorming of ideas written on paper in balloon format. We will be going through each of these items in the following chapters.

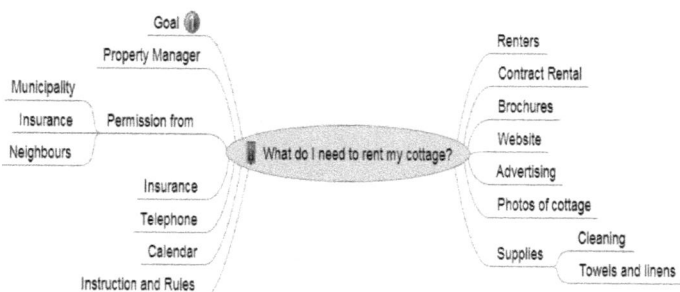

Goal

Property Manager

Municipality

Insurance   Permission from

Neighbours

Insurance

Telephone

Calendar

Instruction and Rules

What do I need to rent my cottage?

Renters

Contract Rental

Brochures

Website

Advertising

Photos of cottage

Cleaning

Supplies

Towels and linens

Chapter 2
Whadda Ya Mean I Can't Rent?

I know this sounds absurd, after all, it is your cottage, but you should find out first if there are any regulations that say you cannot rent out your cottage. Those to consider asking for permission are the municipality, community association, insurance company and don't forget your neighbours.

Municipalities

Some municipalities may not allow you to rent your property. Be sure to check before you start renting. Look in your local blue pages of your telephone book or on the Internet under the city where your cottage is located.

Insurance

While you may have insurance to cover natural disasters and vandalism, not all insurance companies allow you to rent out the property. You need to check with your insurance company to see if you're covered should someone rent your cottage. We cover this in a lot more detail in Chapter 3, page 19 of the book.

Community Associations

The other thing to consider is some cottages have a community association, like a condo corporation where you have to agree to their rules or you may end up paying more to use the common property, especially if you have shared water access or road access. From my experience, they can't tell you what to do on your property, but they can make renting it hard by making renters feel like they are trespassing. I would suggest if you have a community association or shared property of any kid, you contact a lawyer to see what your rights and obligations are. Check with Legal Aid if you can't afford a lawyer.

Neighbours

Now your neighbours are another situation completely different. Don't take them for granted and assume they will be OK with you renting out your property. Some of my neighbours live at their cottage all year and don't want strangers walking around the area. I explained that I am renting my cottage to help pay the mortgage, but that I was screening people so that I didn't get troublemakers. Check to see if there are written rules before you consider renting it. Let your neighbours know what you're doing and if there is a problem with any of the renters, to contact you directly and not bother the renters. A good thing about neighbours too is they will keep an eye out because they don't want trespassers. When I decided to rent my cottage, I put the word out to a few cottage neighbours and they weren't that keen on me doing it because they didn't want strangers around their area. If you decide to rent, just know that not everyone is going to be happy and may cause a few issues with renters, like saying it's not worth the price or there are bears around. Ultimately, it's your property and you are allowed to do with it as you see fit, provided there are no laws restricting you from doing so. Just be respectful of your neighbours and they will help keep your cottage safe as well.

Landlord and Tenant Act

We will not be covering the *Landlord and Tenant Act*. This book is aimed at people renting their cottages on occasion. If you are renting your cottage on a monthly or yearly basis to one person, the Landlord and Tenant Act has different rules. I have provided the links to both Ontario and Quebec boards because they are different provinces with different rules.

Ontario
www.ltb.gov.on.ca/en/STEL02_111286.html

Quebec
www.cmhc-schl.gc.ca/en/co/reho/yogureho/fola/index.cfm

Chapter 3
Protecting Your Investment

Protecting your cottage means ensuring your cottage is safe and should anything happen, you, your cottage and your renters are covered. The following chapter will discuss listing your assets, insurance coverage, how to add protection from fire and carbon dioxide and how to deal with unwelcome guests.

List of Assets

List your assets both inside and outside the cottage so that if something goes missing or gets broken, you can discuss it with the renters. Remember, you have their deposit, so they will want to make sure that nothing gets broken.

If you ever put a claim in for damages your insurance company may ask for a list of all the assets. You may need to take photos and provide them to your insurance company with a detailed description. Check with your insurance company to find out what the requirements are should you ever have to put in a claim i.e. pictures of items, description and year purchased may be needed.

The list of assets would be a good document to have included with the rental contract that you have the renters sign. I wouldn't suggest you have a whole lot of details for the contract list. Have something like the item and a comment column beside it for the renter to write feedback or put an OK to say it's in good working order. This too would also be good because if something is not working, they will let you know and you can fix it before the next renter comes in.

NOTE: Take note, things go missing or get broken when renting, it's just par for the course. So, if you have something that is valuable, I recommend you don't keep it at the cottage.

Here's a list of items that you may have.

36' Panasonic TV	3 Blankets, 2 sleeping bags
Sony DVD player	5 Linens (double size)
Carpet area rug - beige floral pattern	6 Pillows, 5 throw pillows
VCR (yes, they still exist)	10 Curtain panels, 5 rods, 5 rolling blinds
Couch - 3 seater red leather	5 Pots, 2 pans
2 Chairs - red leather	50 pieces plastic food containers
Coffee table	2 sets of 12 utensils
2 End Tables	6 Lawn chairs
DVD & VCR Movies (list them separately) **NOTE:** It's also good for the renters so they know what movies you have and which ones belong to them.	Books (list each one separately)
Double bed	Mountain Bike

2 Night tables	Painting of a woman
2 Single beds	BBQ – propane tank (2 tanks if you have them)
Bunk bed	Lawn mower (electric/gas)

What Type of Insurance is Required for My Cottage?

Here's what Rozon Insurance Brokers Ltd had to say:

"Depending on whether your cottage is a Seasonal Dwelling (usually not occupied all year round), a 4 Season cottage, on an island, there are different forms of coverage – from standard/basic coverage to full coverage. Type of coverage is determined by many factors.

The following is information to take into consideration when inquiring about insurance for your cottage:

- Construction and dimensions
- Electrical, plumbing, roof, heating source, wood stoves
- Outbuildings (i.e.: boat houses, bunkies)
- Fire protection (i.e.: distance to closest responding fire hall)
- Claim history
- Access to cottage
- Use of cottage (i.e.: seasonal closing, # of months closed)
- Do you rent?"

Three Types of Insurance

There are three different types of insurance you need to consider when you own and when you are renting your property. There is property or home insurance, content insurance and rental insurance.

1. **Property or Home Insurance**

   Property insurance protects against accidents like downed trees, ice storms, floods, and if you request it, vandalism if you own the property. Make sure that your insurance has this listed on your home insurance. Be careful, some insurance companies will charge you extra for this type of insurance.

2. **Content Insurance**

   Content insurance protects what's inside the property from loss due to fire or vandalism, i.e. jewellery, furniture, paintings, electronics, etc. Rozon Insurance Brokers says that "Your cottage and belongings are covered for the perils as defined in your policy. Perils are events such as fire, water damage, and damage caused by bears. Coverage differs with different insurance companies – make sure your broker explains what coverage you are and are not entitled to. Make sure that you are clear on what coverage you can obtain – burglary, vandalism & malicious act coverage is an additional premium on some policy forms."

3. **Cottage Rental Insurance (a.k.a. Seasonal Policy)**

   So the one big question, does my cottage insurance cover me if I rent out my cottage and it gets damaged? Rozon Insurance Brokers advised that most insurance companies will not provide coverage until either an agent has inspected the property, and/or the owner has completed a questionnaire and provided photos. They also say "Seasonal policy coverage is required when rented to others. Again, check with your respective insurance companies. Some insurance companies say that the cottage must be used by the owners at least 50% of the time."

Before going out and getting insurance, here's some questions I found online at Canadian Cottage Insurance that asks owners 10 very important questions about your policy. (Canadian Cottage Insurance. Date n/a. Web. Retrieved from www.canadiancottageinsurance.com/cottage-checklist.asp)

- Does your current insurance policy provide adequate coverage to replace the building if it was completely destroyed?
- Does your current policy include Replacement Cost on the building?
- Do you understand all policy conditions from your current insurer, including whether you need regular visits to the cottage throughout the year?
- Is your cottage covered for collapse caused by the weight of ice and snow?
- Are you protected against both theft and vandalism?
- Would your contents claim be settled on: the cost to replace the item with something new (replacement cost) or the value of the old item (actual cash value)?
- Is $1,000,000 enough liability coverage to protect you?
- If you decided to rent your cottage for a week would your current policy cover you?
- If your cottage is on an island or remote location, does your policy cover the increased cost of debris removal and bringing in new materials should you suffer a fire loss?
- What coverage is available for your dock?

Where Can I find Cottage Rental Insurance?

There are a few insurance companies I found that offer cottage rental insurance. Do your homework and search out which company offers rental insurance and don't just take the first one. Make sure you get the right coverage for you and your property.

I have listed three companies below that offer cottage insurance in Ontario and Quebec.

Canadian Cottage Insurance (Rozon Insurance Brokers Ltd)
www.canadiancottageinsurance.com
1-800-263-3186

Cooperators
www.cooperatorsgroupinsurance.ca/Other_Products/Seasonal_Home_insurance/
1-800-387-1963

CAA (Canadian Automobile Association)
www.caasco.com/Insurance/Home-Insurance/Cottage-Insurance.aspx
1-888-285-6428

To learn more or find different insurance companies, visit www.insuranceincanada.com.

NOTE: If you don't get rental insurance, which some people don't, I strongly suggest you make sure when you are renting your cottage you get a cheque for damage deposit. This way, should something happen at the cottage, you are at least covered a bit and your renters will be more prudent because they will want their deposit back.

Rozon Insurance Brokers advises that if you do rent your cottage, you should disclose this to the insurance company covering your cottage. Different insurance companies have different guidelines for cottages being rented.

A $40 Investment Could Save You Thousands

A smoke detector, a fire extinguisher and a carbon dioxide (CO_2) detector are three very important things you should have in your cottage and here's why. This may sound obvious to some of you, but it wasn't for me. When I bought the cottage, I didn't even think to look for a smoke detector or fire extinguisher. I was just too excited. However, when you smoke yourself out because you didn't open the wood stove vent and are waiting for an alarm to go off as it would at home, you realize...oops, need a smoke detector.

Your renters may like to cook French fries, and while you may not have a fryer in the cottage, people could still cook with oil using a simple pot. If the oil spills on the floor, it could cause a fire and people panic and throw water on grease which in turn spreads the fire. Where if you had a fire extinguisher in the kitchen, they could use it right away and save you thousands of dollars in damages.

If there is CO_2 in the cottage, it could potentially kill a person. I found online from ehow.com that "If there is too much carbon dioxide gas in the air, a person could die of hypercapnia, a condition in which there is too high a build-up of carbon dioxide in the blood" (April Sanders. Date: n/a Web. Retrieved from: www.ehow.com/how-does_4695252_carbon-dioxide-poisoning-kill-human_.html).

If you're using a wood stove, there are gases that emit from burning wood that you can't see or even smell, but this is one thing that causes CO_2.

There are a few sites I listed below that warn you of the symptoms and ways to protect your cottage and yourself from getting sick.

Health Canada
www.hc-sc.gc.ca/hl-vs/iyh-vsv/environ/wood-bois-eng.php

eHow
How Does Carbon Dioxide Poisoning Kill a Human?
www.ehow.com/how-does_4695252_carbon-dioxide-poisoning-kill-human_.html#ixzz26B3BzA00

Canadian Centre for Occupational Health and Safety
www.ccohs.ca/oshanswers/chemicals/chem_profiles/carbo n_dioxide/health_cd.html

Where can I buy these items?

You can find the CO_2 smoke detector and fire extinguisher at most hardware stores like Canadian Tire, Home Depot or Rona. They cost about $40 and could save you thousands of dollars in property damage, and possibly save someone's life because they were able to detect the danger.

Unwelcome Guests – Mice, Animals and Bugs

The cottage is in the woods and the woods are nature where mice, bugs and other animals live. We would prefer they stay outside of the cottage, but sometimes they manage to get in. So, what do you need to do if you have a problem? Take care of it before you start renting and here's how.

Mice are cute and fuzzy...NOT!!! I know we don't like to talk about the negative things of your lovely cottage, but let's be real. It could have mice. It is after all the country.

If you have mice, here are some suggestions, but keep in mind, until all possible entries into the cottage have been blocked, this may be a recurring problem. Here are two possible solutions to eliminate the mice. Get rid of them yourself, or pay an exterminator.

Option 1 - Get rid of them yourself

First thing is to keep your cottage clean at all times. Mice love food, just like we do, especially sweets. Store your food in sealed jars or tins. Look for holes around doors, windows, cracks in walls. Seal all openings that would allow a mouse to get it. Take note, they can get in a hole the size of a dime.

Here's a list of products I have tried and got results.

- Scotch Steel Scourer pads (seal the holes with this metal as they don't seem to like it because it cuts them)
- Mothballs (they seem to help keep them away, but you end up finding all these white balls around and, if you have pets or kids, they might stick them in their mouth which is dangerous)
- Mouse traps or snap traps (www.victorpest.com/store/mouse-control/snap-traps)

- Plastic Traps (Victor Quick Set Mouse Trap). Put peanut butter on it because they really like it. The only problem with this is that you have to clean it up after and throw out the mouse.
- Ratol Rat Bait Pellets (www.homehardware.ca). I like this one because they disintegrate and all you have to do is throw out the bones. I know, it's not pleasant, but better this than the full body and smell that comes with it.
- Peppermint oil (I haven't tried it as I don't like the smell of peppermint. You can buy it at any health food store).
- Noise plugin (Victor UltraSonic Mini Pest). I used it, but I didn't see a difference because I still found mouse droppings in the kitchen drawers.

Most of these products can be found at Canadian Tire, Rona and Home Hardware, and in Quebec there's also BMR.

IMPORTANT: If a renter finds a mouse and no longer wishes to stay at your cottage, this may be a reason for them to break the contract and you will have to return their payment.

Option 2 - Hire a professional pest control specialist

If you prefer not to deal with the issues or the issue requires professional services, hire a professional. You can also search the Internet under pest control specialist or wildlife removal and you should find a few. Also the Yellow Pages have listings.

Here are two professionals that I have heard of:

Pest Guard – www.pestguard.ca

Abell Pest Control - www.abellpestcontrol.com

Chapter 4
How Much Can I Charge?

In order to know what you can charge, you must know the following:

- What are my expenses now and when I have renters?
- Who is my competition?
- What is my goal?

What Are My Expenses Now Versus With Renters?

Your current expenses are the things that happen on a monthly basis that you must take into consideration when renting. They include:

- Mortgage
- Utilities (electricity, gas, water)
- Maintenance (grass cutting, snow removal, buying wood, road maintenance, propane tank for BBQ)
- Property taxes

When you start renting, you will also need to calculate on top of the current expenses things like:

- Adverting fees if you place ads in print and online, which I strongly recommend you do. Otherwise, how will people know your cottage exists?
- Fees associated with web hosting and domain name that you pay every year.
- Utilities (electric baseboards, gas and hot water). Contact your utility company to see what your bills are in a month that you were there every weekend or the times you were there a week or two and use those numbers.

- If you have a wood stove or fireplace, you will need to purchase more wood, depending if you rent in winter and fall.
- Propane or coals for the BBQ.
- Cleaning supplies and equipment such as a vacuum and a mop.

For my cottage, it's about a 10% increase in those months, as I didn't have a washer/dryer or a stove. If you use the stove a lot or have air conditioning and a dryer, then consider 15-20% as they consume a lot of energy, not to mention hot water tanks too as we women like to take hot showers, or at least I do and can be in there for half an hour at times.

NOTE: Summer months versus winter are completely different as you are not inside as much using things like heat, stove and lights. So, be sure to average out the yearly expense.

What Form Of Payment Do I Accept?

So, now you have people who want to rent your cottage, what form of payment system are you going to use? The methods available out there to use include: certified cheque or money order, cash, email money transfer, Paypal, and credit cards. Take into consideration that there are fees for some of these services. I personally prefer money order, email money transfer, or cash because you get the deposit right away and don't have to worry about bounced cheques or credit card fees.

Contact your bank or lending institution to see what are your options, how much it costs and how long they take to process these payments. I would list them here, but some banks do things differently and I don't want to confuse you.

Credit Card Payments

Credit card payment is another good form of payment because you are guaranteed payment, but there are admin fees with this service. There are a few companies that accept credit cards on your behalf if you don't have a business account.

- Intuit – www.merchantservices.intuit.ca/payment-processing/intuit-merchant-service-for-quickbooks.jsp
- Moneris – www.moneris.com
- Pivotal Payments - www.pivotalpayments.com/ca/en/

PayPal

PayPal is an e-commerce business that lets you take credit card or online payments and money transfers via the Internet. The best part is they don't have administrative fees like the credit cards and your bank. They do, however, charge you per transaction. Visit their website at www.personal.paypal.com/ca.

What Do I Have That Really Attracts People To My Cottage?

Now that you have the base of your expenses, it's time see what makes your cottage stand out from the rest. Consider these things when deciding on a price, as people are willing to pay more for them.

- Are you waterfront or access to water and is it a beach or weedy area? Waterfront seems to be something you can charge a higher price for compared to just water access that is not really private.
- How close are you to a major city?
- Do you have sun exposure or are there many trees around that hide the sun from getting in?

- Are you on an island that requires boat to get to it, making it less appealing for those without a boat?
- Do you have extras like washer/dryer, a hot tub, more bedrooms, etc.?

People are willing to pay more for these things. I know this because I am one of them who will pay more for things like hot tub. If you don't have neighbors on each side, this is another thing that people may be willing to pay a higher price for.

Who Is My Competition?

Your competition in this case is other cottages in the area and around other towns. You need to see what Joe down the street is charging as well as the other cottages in the next town over. Your goal is to make money, but not have your cottage overpriced or you may not have enough renters to meet your financial goal.

Ask a few property rental companies to see what the going rates for cottages are in your area.

Look at the cottage rentals listed online and the stores in and around your cottage area to see what others are charging. Walk around and visit other cottages, talk to neighbours, compare sizes, is it a 3- or 4-season, what are the features and compare prices with yours. Be objective!

Here's an example of what I did to find out who my competition was: I searched the internet for "cottages for rent Ottawa" and found links to website that list many cottages. I took the first 3 search pages I found because there were over 10,000 (People usually only look at the first 3 pages on the web. If they can't find the information, they change their search criteria). The cottages I found online were on average 1,000 square feet, where mine is 500 square feet. They had waterfront where mine only has water access. They could accommodate 6 to 12 people, where mine could sleep 4 comfortably. They were on a big lake; mine was on a quiet one with no motorboats. The average price for 1-week rental was $700 to $2,000. So, I couldn't charge what the bigger cottages were charging because my cottage is a simple, small and an older cottage that didn't have all those features like washer/dryer, hot tub, and waterfront. I had to identify what was different about my cottage, not better, just what makes it a cottage that people would want to rent. The one feature I have was that there are only 17 cottage owners on this private lake that only allowed electric boats, which means peace and quiet.

What Formula Do I Use To Make A Profit?

To get my rates I took the average rental price of my competition of $700 weekly. I found this average price when searching the web for cottages around my area with similar features. I reduced it by $100 because I didn't have all the features that the other cottages were charging such as waterfront.

Here's a breakdown of the costs:

- Monthly expenses:
    - mortgage
    - utilities
    - taxes
    - community fees
    - advertising
    - association fee
    - septic tank disposal
    - maintenance
    - cleaners/supplies

- 10% increase in utilities + natural gas or propane for BBQ
- Bank or credit card transaction fees (I only took cash or cheque as I didn't want to pay the bank administrative fees.)

Here's an example of my monthly cost calculation:

Average weekly rental ($700 -$100)	$600
Minus monthly expenses	- $415
Minus 10% increase in bills	- $ 41
Total Profit	**= $141**

That is just for one week's rental a month. I had another advantage with my cottage: I rented weekends too, which not too many cottages offered at a lower rate. I found I had more renters who wanted weekends, whereas families want them for the week.

To cover my monthly expenses, I needed 2 weekend rentals per month to cover the basic expenses. Again I did a Google search and found the average price for weekends was $500. Based on what my cottage had to offer, I charged $350 and people paid for it, which gave me bigger profit. If you price too low, you might get the wrong kind of renters. This price seemed to be a fair one and I got many renters.

Here's a breakdown of the potential profit I could make for a year:

Total income for weekend rentals for 12 months (assuming it is rented every weekend)

$350 X 53 weekends in year = **$18,200**

Total expenses for 12 months

($415 + $41) x 12 months = **$5,472**

Potential profit after 12 months

$18,200 - $5,472 = **$12,728**

What About the Months I Can't Rent?

If your cottage is a 3-season i.e. not insulated or road not accessible in winter, there is a chance you may not make back that money for your expenses and your goal. You need to consider the expenses for the period you don't rent it, which is usually November to March. So, you need to expose yourself to as many renters as possible during the times you are able to rent. What you could do to make up some of that time is charge more during the holidays like long weekends. July to September is the busy season. Charge more for things like long weekends or special holidays like Canada Day.

People are willing to pay more to do something fun during their holidays and the seasons seem to have different peaks as well. Here are the seasons to look at and charge different rates accordingly.

> May - June (spring)
>
> July - August (summer)
>
> September - October (fall)
>
> November – April (winter)

NOTE: Be careful, if you price too high, you may not get as many renters and your cottage could sit empty, which means more lost revenue. You also don't want to be too low as your goal is to make a profit.

Don't forget the goal. In Chapter 1, you identified what your goal was for renting the cottage. When calculating the formula, make sure to add your goal into the price. I have provided you with my goal and showed you the formula. My goal was to have monthly bills paid and I did that and made profit, which I used to make improvements to the cottage such as a new deck and a kitchen floor.

Chapter 5
Dealing with Renters

When you rented cottages before you bought your own, there were things the owners did to protect their cottage and ensure you enjoyed your stay. This section will cover those things that you need to do as well like

- Rental agreement contracts
- Rules and instructions on use of equipment
- Location of supplies
- Method of payment
- Damage deposit
- Handing over the keys

Rental Agreement Contract

To protect yourself and your renters, have them sign a rental agreement contract. A rental agreement contract has the renters personal details, what is included with the rental, the rules for using the cottage and how to reach you in case of emergency, and what the renter is responsible for during and after their stay.

The contract should include the following information:

- Personal information about the renters and their guests i.e. full name of renters and other people staying in the cottage, age of renters, home address, telephone (work, cell, and home), name of employer, address of employer, driver's license, car's make and model and license plate

- Rules for using the cottage i.e. number of guests allowed, fishing license, outdoor fire.

- When payment is due and amount of damage deposit.

- Who to contact in case of emergency.

- Damage deposit: what date you require it, the condition to getting it back.

- Keys: when to pick them up and drop them off.

- Liability information such as swim at their own risk.

- Arrival/Departure times: When they can arrive and what time they must vacate.

- Inspection: Have them do a walk-around to see if there is any damage before they stay. This may scare some of them, but better to be safe than sorry and have them complete an Incident Report. What they are responsible for i.e. cleaning, vacuum, putting patio furniture away, removing their food from fridge/freezer and cleaning it, remove of garbage and recycling removal and location.

- Kitchen supplies: make sure to tell them to bring plastic containers, plastic wrap, tin foil, and napkins.

- Outdoor fire pit: What wood do they use and when can they actually light the fire, e.g. due to weather and by-laws at certain times of the year, you may not permitted to light outdoor fires. Fire wood: do you provide it or do the renters have to buy it and if so, where can they get it.

- Pets: If you don't want them, make the renters initial they agree no pets so that if you find out there were animals at the cottage, you can keep the deposit to fix the damage, if any.

- Cancellation Refund: Add in your contract the minimum number of days' notice required for a refund for the rental. You can have a "no cancellation" policy, but this will limit the amount of possible renters

What the Renters Need to Bring

Make sure you advise the renters what's included and what they need to bring to the cottage to make their stay pleasurable and one they'll brag to their friends about. Provide a list of things that are not included like:

- toilet paper
- dish soap
- toiletries
- first aid kit
- paper towels
- plastic containers for food (they do take them, so if you supply them, know you'll need to replace them)
- towels
- soap
- insect repellent
- blankets
- pillows
- fishing license
- boat
- gas for propane tank or boat

Incident Report

You should have in the contract an Incident Report. An Incident Report is a list of what the renter noticed as damaged and lets you know so they and you are aware and take action to fix it.

Have the renters do their own walk around and take note of what's been damaged and advise you of such. Asked them to complete an Incident Report and return it with the keys.

The report should include the following:

- Name of renter
- Date of rental
- Location or item damaged
- Details of the damage (example: top kitchen drawer handle missing a screw)
- Signature of renter

NOTE: Check after every rental to see what needs to be replenished like dish soap, cleaning supplies, mop and broom.

Method of Contacting You

You will need a method for people to contact you that includes a telephone, voicemail, and an email account.

Voice Mail or Answering Machine

Your telephone company can offer voice mail service. It's about $5 to $7 per month, or you can purchase an answering machine for about $40 at Canadian Tire or Wal-Mart that works just as well. The disadvantage to an answering machine is if you're on the telephone, they can't leave a message. Either way you need one so that renters can leave you their request.

Emails

People will enquire about your cottage usually by email based from online ads you posted. To answer emails, you need an email program like MS Outlook, Gmail, Hotmail, or Yahoo. Most of these are free programs you can download to your computer.

I have a Gmail account and love it because I can access it from anywhere in the world that has an Internet connection. Not to mention, it's has lots of FREE software to help you write your contracts and email replies.

With email, you can keep track of who contacted you and add their contact details to your rental database that you should be building. This information can then be used later when you're doing a promotion or sale, or last minute rental.

NOTE: <u>DO NOT SPAM people!!!</u> If they don't want to receive email from you, don't contact them. Not to mention there are laws about spamming. Check out the link from Industry Canada to learn more:

www.ic.gc.ca/eic/site/ecic-ceac.nsf/eng/gv00521.html.

Instructions and Rules for Use of the Cottage

To make the stay for the renters more enjoyable, have a list of instructions on how to use the electronics like DVD, CD, TV, or how to open the vent to start the fire in the wood stove. I know the first time I had to light a fire in the wood stove, I smoked myself out of the cottage...hee hee...I was such a city slicker who never lit a fire.

When you rent, there could be a fuse that gets blown, or light bulbs burn out. You need to let the renters know where to find them, and make sure you have them stored at the cottage.

Here are some things you may want to consider providing instructions for:

- BBQ propane or charcoal
- wood stove
- TV & DVD player
- toaster oven
- heating system like baseboard heaters
- replacing fuses and where to find them
- outdoor fire pit
- toilet (environmental ones have different flush mechanisms)
- location of supplies i.e. light bulbs, fuses, candles, wood for stove, etc.

Rules are meant as a guideline to avoid things going wrong and keeping neighbors and renters happy. Here are some examples: no pets in the cottage or at the dock or beach area, especially if it's a shared dock, no smoking inside or on the patio, no campfire except in sealed fire pit, clean up after you leave. You can include the rules in the instructions or add to rental agreement.

Have a copy of instruction/rules located somewhere visible like on the fridge with a magnet or on the kitchen table.

Cleaning the Cottage

If you decide to have renters clean the cottage, have a list of what they need to clean. The list should be attached to the rental agreement and another copy left on the fridge or somewhere visible. The list should also tell the renters where they could find the cleaning supplies. You should be very specific as not everyone cleans the same way.

Here's a short list of what I have on my rules:

- sweep and mop floors (specify the rooms)
- clean bathroom (sink, shower, toilet)
- kitchen (wipe counters, put dishes away)
- garbage removal and disposal at the dump
- vacuuming rugs, stairs, carpets and around the fireplace

Receipts for Rentals

When you have received payment from renters, you will need to provide them with a receipt. If you ask for a damage deposit and payment, you should write out a receipt for both the rental payment and damage deposit, so that you don't confuse the payments and can easily identify which ones must be returned to the renter. The receipt will need to be given to the renter after they paid.

Things you need to include on your receipt are:

- Your first and last name, cottage name (if applicable)
- Telephone, email, and website address (if applicable)
- Receipt number (they must be unique & in order)
- Renter name
- Date of rental
- Amount paid
- Method of payment (cash, check, money order, credit card)
- Today's date
- Signature
- Comments: such as "receipt for rental/deposit"

You can get free templates to use for receipts from Microsoft at: www.wordtemplatesonline.com

Damage Deposit Cheque Return

The cheque for damage deposit should be returned usually one week after you have inspected the cottage to make sure nothing was damaged or stolen. You know that some things get damaged with different people using the cottage, so take that into consideration when you do the inspection and you shouldn't charge for things like stains on carpet, scratches on wood floor, glasses being broken, but...this is up to you.

You should also let them know when they can expect to have their deposit returned. It's usually within a week of the rental.

Handing Over the Keys

Once the contract is signed and payment made in full, now it's time to give the keys to the renters. Make sure you have an extra set or two, just in case they lose them. Set up a time to meet the renters to pick up and drop off the keys.

Chapter 6
Keep On Top of Your Rentals
and Your Goals

There are two important things you need for your cottage:

- a calendar for bookings
- monthly sales report

Calendar for Bookings

A calendar is very important to help you keep track of all your rentals as well as when deposits are to be returned and when you have to pay the government their taxes. You can use a simple wall hanging one, but I prefer to use a weekly planner because it has more room to write details and I can carry it with me at all times so that if a prospect calls, I can let them know the available dates.

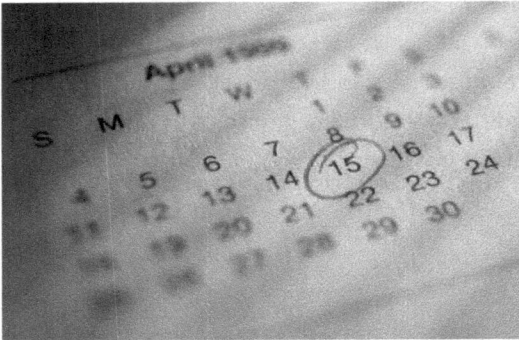

Things to keep track of include:

- name
- telephone
- email
- dates requested
- comments: such as call back time or when you called them back so that you know you followed up, date they called or if they rented and they were or were not good renters.

If you have your own website or have your information on an online rental company, make sure to have a calendar on the website to show people available dates and to avoid people calling you for already booked dates. However, you could also have a cancellation list for those that want certain dates or last minute specials on your website on the calendar page.

Monthly Sales and Your Goal

In chapter 1, we identified what your goal was. Now you need to keep an eye on your sales to see where you're at with your goal and what, if any, action steps you need to take to reach your target. I do this by reviewing my monthly sales and yearly sales to see when i rent the most times and find ways to increase sales or up my price during the months that are not busy.

In the next section, I have listed my sales for the year 2011.

Yearly Sales Report 2011

Jan	$0
Feb	$0
March	$0
April	$250
May	$600
June	$1,600
July	$2,500
August	$2,500
September	$1,200
October	$1,000
November	$0
December	$0

Chapter 7
What Makes My Cottage Special

Now you are ready to start finding renters, but how do you go about it? First off, you need to know what type of renters you want, what the renters are looking for in a cottage and how you are going to advertise your cottage.

Who Do You Want Renting Your Cottage?

Deciding and identifying the type of renters you want is extremely important. Believe me, I learned very fast. I accepted anyone who wanted to rent my cottage, as long as they paid and had a job, that's all I cared about. Pay attention to your gut!!! People can be irresponsible when it's not their place.

Do you want to rent to people like you who will respect and treat the cottage like it was their own home, or do you want ones like the neighbours you dislike? Be willing to say NO to those people that just don't fit your profile of a good renter, and if your gut says NO, then you may want to listen. I didn't listen and learned the hard way. I found out from my neighbours that one group of renters had allowed BIG dogs in the cottage when I said and wrote in the contract no dogs, and they broke my bed and didn't tell me about it. Needless to say, it cost me money, but I learned that my gut said they are not the right renters.

Make a list of the ideal renter

Think of it this way: who would be the ideal roommate, if you were picking one? So try writing a want ad first, then change it into a Rental Agreement.

Age: I chose 25. I wanted adults as I didn't want my cottage to be a party place and get trashed. While I had fun at 25, I thought I was mature at that age. Besides, they would need to provide a deposit should anything break. I don't know many people under 25 who have extra money.

Pets: I say no to pets. For me, I'm allergic to dog and cat hair and cleaning up after them is too much work. Not to mention some may chew things like furniture.

Smoking: I don't like the smell, and trying to get that smell out means I have to wash everything. So, I said no. Not to mention the fact that they can cause fires and burn holes in the carpet, on floor or worse, your bed!

Children: Do they have any, if so what age? My cottage was not suitable for kids.

Employed: I wanted to be sure that if anything happened, I had a way to get a hold of the renter through their employer.

Lifestyle: Quiet versus party types.

Extra Guest: If a renter asks for one more guest to be added at no cost, you can either say yes or charge extra. It's the norm to have an extra fee for additional guests.

References: You may want to ask if they have references from previous places they rented. Not many people ask for this, and you may push people away if you are too picky, but again, it's your choice.

Defining these questions will also help you to create your ad because you'll now be able to describe who would enjoy your cottage.

Describing the Cottage

Do you need a description of your cottage when you are looking to rent it? That answer MUST be yes even for your friends and family! People looking to rent will have questions and will always want to see pictures. When you have finished describing it, you will use the details you created to post on your own website or online rental websites, as well as free Internet advertising.

So, what makes a good description? Paint a picture, set the mood or be factual and precise.

Here are a few ways to do it. Describe your cottage as you would to your friends; maybe describe the dock and how the sun sets over the water. It will be from your heart and people will feel it. When I look to rent other people's cottages, I look at things like number of people that can sleep comfortably, not too far from the city or driving from Ottawa, has to have a lake to swim in (no weeds...ewwww), things to do around the area (car shows, craft fairs, concerts) toys for the water and outdoors like badminton and water tubes, a full bathroom with shower (not an outhouse), wood stove or fire place, and the bonus that sold me is a hot tub.

Do some research on cottages for rent in your area or what ads get posted at the top of Google.

Ask yourself, would you rent your cottage? The answer must be yes! Now you must answer why would you rent this place? What do you love about the cottage and location? This will give you an idea as to what your renters are looking for. Are they looking for a small, simple place, short drive from the city, on a budget? Maybe waterfront or at least close to water, quiet with not too many neighbours, close to restaurants and town just in case people don't like to cook and like to shop.

Try asking yourself the 5 W questions: Who, What, Where, When and Why.

- Who will stay here? How many people can it fit? Is it kid and pet friendly? Families with kids, adults only?
- What will they do with their time? Fish, swim, read, BBQ, quiet time, family time?
- Where is the cottage? How close to a municipality and the closest city?
- What else is around? How many other cottages are there? Surrounded by trees, family owned cottages?
- Why is it such a great place?
- When is it available? Weekends, monthly, weekly, daily?
- What is the style? Cute, exotic, modern, 5-star, rustic, open-concept, log cabin?
- What size is it? Is it big or small, size of the cottage i.e. 500 square feet?
- What are the architectural features? Large windows, exposed beams, antique light fixtures (NEW)?
- How many bedrooms? 2 bedrooms, master en-suite, hand-made bunk beds, size of the beds i.e. queen, singles?
- What are the number of people it can sleep comfortably? 3 bedrooms, a pull-out couch (This does not mean the floor but rather beds and couches.)
- How many bathrooms and are they full bathrooms? Does it have a sink, bath or shower, and toilet?
- What type of furniture? Is it fully furnished? Describe the furniture like 3-seater leather couch, TV, music, books, DVD movies, washer/dryer, etc.
- What's on the outside of the cottage? Deck, veranda (covered), does it have grass or sand, or rocks, hot tub, swimming pool?

- Is it waterfront or access to water? How far from cottage in feet? Does it face the water? Can you fish or swim in it? How big is the lake? What type of fish? Does it have a sandy beach?
- How is it heated? Wood stove, electric baseboard or gas?
- Is the water system drinkable hot and cold?
- Does it have electricity? Do you have lights? There are cottages that are on islands with no electricity.
- Is it on land or an island? Do you need a boat to get to the cottage? Is a boat supplied?
- What type of kitchen appliances and supplies are there? Fridge, stove or stove-top, toaster, toaster oven, utensils, cleaning supplies, fondue set, wine glasses, pots/pans, martini glasses, places, bowls, etc.?
- How many parking spots can fit on your lot?
- Is there a telephone landline or cell access?
- What is supplied? Linens/blankets/towels, dishtowels, dish soap, cleaning supplies?
- Is there a satellite TV or Internet or DVD player with movies?
- Is there a BBQ? Is it gas or charcoal

Features

What are the features that make your cottage unique or more appealing compared to others?

- **Privacy**: are there neighbors on each side or are they far apart.
- **Season**: is it a 3 or 4-season (4 being winterized and running water in the winter)
- **Washer/dryer**: do you have a washer/dryer on site

- **Location**: where is it actually located, like the name of township, lake, river, etc. Only give the address to confirmed renters on rental agreement so as not to get strangers coming to see your place without permission.

  NOTE: It's important to note who has access rights, right of way on to your property if any. For example: shared lake or dock access.

- **Outdoor fire pit**: is wood supplied?
- **Surroundings**: surrounded by trees, are they family owned cottages or renters?
- **Distance**: close to the city without all the busyness and noise and only 17 neighbours.
- **Nearby attractions:** golf courses, national parks, towns that may have activities, municipal fairs
- **Toys/games**: do you have air mattress, fishing rod, a boat, board games, movies, etc.?
- **Equipment rentals**: Are there boat or bike rental businesses close by.
- **Food and alcohol**: Where is the closest grocery and liquor store

Activities and Local Attractions

Activities make your cottage stand out from the rest. What's around the area to see and do? Include a list of activities around the cottage and in the nearby area. These are the things that make the area sound really interesting. Check out your local grocery store or restaurant and ask them what happens, better yet, contact the local tourism bureau, Chamber of Commerce or municipal office for more information. You can also ask your real estate agent to provide you with some assistance. Ask the local stores as well. Pick up flyers and leave them at the cottage for guests to browse.

Here is a list of activities to consider adding if they are located around your cottage:

- horseback riding
- white water rafting
- canoeing
- kayak
- scuba diving
- biking
- sailing
- garage sales
- recreation vehicle parks
- baseball
- apple, raspberry, strawberry picking
- spa/salon
- car shows
- tasting homemade pies
- church bazaar
- concerts
- lakes
- ocean
- rock climbing
- secret/hidden lake
- festivals
- church
- bakery
- local artist work
- car shows
- golf courses
- fishing
- cricket
- boating
- snowmobiling
- lawn darts
- skiing, snowboarding (downhill, x-country)
- paddle boat
- hunting
- camp site
- geocaching
- outdoor movie theatre
- beaches
- games room (board games, pool table, ping pong, air hockey, pin ball)
- golf tournaments
- fishing tournaments

NOTE: Don't forget to provide the website link or telephone number for these activities so the renters can contact them.

For the outdoor enthusiasts, you could include information on nature and what to do like:

- bird watching
- hiking
- bike trails
- swimming
- tree climbing
- rock climbing
- spelunking

Fishing and Hunting

If there is fishing allowed, what type of fish are there in the lake? Same thing goes for hunting, what can they hunt for. Make sure they know they need to get a fishing and/or hunting license for each province they fish or hunt in as they are NOT transferable.

To get details about your area and the rules for these activities, contact your municipality.

Ontario - Ontario Ministry of Natural Resources:

FISHING
www.mnr.gov.on.ca/en/Business/LetsFish/2ColumnSubPage/STEL02_164832.html

HUNTING
www.mnr.gov.on.ca/en/Business/FW/2ColumnSubPage/STEL02_168421.html

Quebec - Resources naturelles et faune:

FISHING
www.mrnf.gouv.qc.ca/english/publications/online/wildlife/fishing-regulations/regles-generales/fishing-licence.asp

HUNTING
www.mrnf.gouv.qc.ca/english/publications/online/wildlife/hunting-regulations/index.asp

Liabilities for "Toys"

If you are renting your cottage with electrical toys such as motor boat or ATV, make sure you contact your insurance company to see if you are in fact covered for damages that may be caused to other properties as well as to the renters themselves.

Have renters sign a liability form that states if they or their guests get hurt, you are not responsible and they cannot sue you.

Here's a link to a sample template that you can and should modify to protect you and the renters.

www.cfsa.org/selfinsure/genlib/release_waivers.htm

Photos

Everyone wants to see what they're getting. Photos take people into your property without you having to show them in person.

You need to show people what your cottage looks like both inside and out, so take pictures of the best features and place them with your advertisement. You can double the interest in your ad by providing photos.

If you really want to get the best look for your cottage, you may want to consider hiring a professional photographer. You can also hire a student from your local community college or private school.

This photo was taken by *Chris Dunlop* with a Canon Professional camera.

NOTE: When you're downloading photos make sure you change the pixels to 600 x 300, or you may not be able to upload the photos.

Chapter 8
Getting the Word Out

There are many ways to find renters, but the question is what type of advertising do you want use and how much time and money you can devote to each of them. Before you decide which place to advertise, you will need to write an ad about your cottage.

How to Write Your Ad

When you are looking to rent a cottage, what is the first thing you look for in the ad? For me it's always waterfront or access to a lake. When you're writing your ad, think about all the features your cottage has and the renters you're trying to attract. Don't forget to include pictures of your cottage or lake so people can see and feel what it would be like to stay there.

Here's a sample of what my ad looks like.

<u>2-bedroom cottage - 1 hour from Ottawa</u>

Cozy 2-bedroom cottage just outside the city of Ottawa in the town of Cheneville Quebec. Perfect for a couple looking to get away for the weekend or for small family of 4. Enjoy the quietness of the woods, take a swim in the beautiful lake that has no motor boats, get a massage just up the street, or go see the local artist show. Don't feel like cooking? There are 3 restaurants just a 5-minute drive away. It has everything you need just like at home, only without the business.

Don't wait, book TODAY as weekends get booked up fast! Go to www.tinalalonde.webs.com.

Look at other cottage rental ads online or flyers you may have seen. Use some of their information to help you write your ad. Ask your friends, family or colleagues when they are searching online what words they use to search.

Software to Help You Write Ads

You will need to use software to write your ads to post online. Most computers come with software called Notepad or Text. Now, if you want to make things look more professional, maybe add pictures, you will need software that allow modifications and image uploads. Not to worry, Google offers free tools in their Google Docs once you create an email account with them. They have the following: word processing, spreadsheets, presentations, forms, web pages.

26 Ways and Places to Advertise

1.   Business Cards

When you meet someone, you should always have a way for people to find out about your business. So have your business cards and/or brochures ready. A business card and brochure is a way to tell people about your cottage, where they can find out more information about it and how to contact you to book a rental.

You should have the following information on the card:

- your first and last name
- name of your cottage
- telephone
- email
- website address or link to cottage rental site that you advertise on
- picture of your cottage or lake

NOTE: Vistaprint offers free business cards www.vistaprint.com and all you have to pay for is the shipping fee of about $10.00.

2. Brochure

A brochure is an 8 ½ x 11 page that folds in 3. It allows for a short description of the cottage you're offering. You can put pictures of what the cottage or the lake looks like, the area, and list some of the local attractions people can do while at your cottage. You would usually ask a grocery store and local restaurant or business if you can leave a few copies. Make sure you have a holder to put them in. You should also check after every visit to the cottage to replenish them, so that there will always be a brochure available for new renters.

3. Posters

A poster is similar to a brochure in that it's 8 ½" by 11" paper, but can be much larger. You could put them up all around your town, library, or posts outside. Ask permission first from the city if you can put posters up on the posts.

4. Friends and Family

Tell your friends and family about your plans to rent your cottage. You may be surprised that they may want to rent it from you. As well, they may know someone who is looking and will tell them about your cottage. Maybe even ask them if they can post the ad at their office or local church or community centre. You have nothing to lose by asking and so much to gain. Don't forget to thank them or better yet, get them a gift when you get a referral from them, something like a gift certificate to Tim Horton's or LCBO.

5. Colleagues/Work

Let your colleagues at work know you have a cottage that you are renting and ask them if they'd be willing to help spread the word to their friends to see if they know of anyone who might be interested in renting. Hand out your business card or brochure (if you're allowed) and tell them about any specials you may have. People love deals!

6. Work Ads

Some employers allow you to post your own personal ads of things for sale or services you offer, just as long as it doesn't conflict with your work. Look at your internal intranet to see something called bulletin board, want ads, or maybe you have a corkboard in your cafeteria that you can hang your brochure or business card or special deals poster.

7. Newspaper Ads

Do you remember the days when you were looking to rent an apartment? The words didn't always make sense, so you called to find out more details. Ads were 2 lines that read 2 bdrm, fully furnished. This meant 2 bedroom fully furnished. The ads cost you $35 for 1 week. Well, they are still a good source but there are much better sources. Look at local newspapers in the city you live.

8. Online Classifieds Ads

Now with the internet, online classified ads allow you to describe the many benefits of your property. You can create free ads online. Also search online for words like "free advertising" because new companies come up all the time.

9. Google Maps (Free)

Place your cottage address postal code on Google maps for free. Google links address places first before other articles. **Go to www.google.ca/places** to get instructions on how to post your cottage details.

10. Newsletter or Blog

A newsletter or blog is another great way to get free advertising. A newsletter or blog is a regular publication that is distributed to people interested in information you are offering. It's a good way to let people know of events going on around town or if you have a deal going on.

There are too many people offering information on how to write the best newsletter or blog, so I will leave this to you to search on the internet "how to write a newsletter or blog" and use the one that meets your needs.

11. Radio and Television

The radio and television are another source for advertising, but they can get very costly. There are too many to list in this book. Do a search on the internet under local radio and TV stations in Ontario and Quebec. Also, check to see if you can offer your cottage rental as a prize to their audience. This will get you lots of exposure.

12. Website

Best way I found to get people was to create my own website and link it to the places where I placed advertisements. A website offered me more space to add the benefits to renting your cottage, you can add more pictures of all the land and inside and out, and specials when you offer them.

You can build an easy one, get a professional site, or build a free one, but the free one puts their own ads on it and sometimes it's other cottages. I have more details on building websites later in the chapter.

13. Affiliates

Affiliates are like referrals. For every rental you get because someone you know told a renter about your cottage, you give them a finder's fee. Ask the renter how they found your cottage. These are usually on websites.

Add a line to your contract for affiliates, call it "referred by" so that you can keep track of who gives you more referrals and get them a nice gift at the end of the year to show them how much you appreciate all they did to help you rent your cottage. Don't forget to send a personal card and thank you.

14. Newspaper article

You could write an article for the paper about the area where your cottage is located, maybe let people know of a special event coming up and what it's like to take part in these events. In return, they might advertise your cottage ad information for free.

Again, there are too many people offering information on how to write articles, so do your own search on writing articles and get information about the event or location you want to write about. Also, you should ask a librarian. They are a wonderful source of information.

15. Trade shows

A trade show is an event that allows business owners to display their product or services. They have them in most cities and specialized ones for cottage, but the booth rental is quite costly.

I would suggest you partner with another company that is not in direct competition, or advertise your cottage with a company that attends these events.

16. Coupons Online

The new big craze is online coupons. You simply register through a local dealer, tell them your price and for every booking sold, they get 50%. There is no upfront fee for you. You don't make a lot of money from coupons but it's not about that, it's about getting the word out about your property, and believe me, the word spreads pretty fast. You can set the number of rental coupons you are selling so as not to get completely booked and not make much profit. The idea is to get the word out about your cottage.

I found these websites just to name a few. Some of them only serve certain cities, so you will need to do some searching to find out which one you want to advertise with. You can either choose one specific coupon company or one that copies all the deals from each of the coupon companies. Each of them has their own database of people looking for deals, but if you're like most people you don't want to sign up for 10 deals.

Here's a list of those I found with vacation deals.

www.mydealbag.com/roster/sites/ottawa
www.dealfind.com
www.DealCanada.ca
www.Groupon.ca
www.KijijiDailyDeals.com
www.LivingDeal.com
www.LivingSocial.com

NOTE: If you sign up for any of these through my website www.howtorentmycottage.ca, I will pay you 50% of the commission of what they paid me to have you sign up. So, you get deals from them and you get paid from me. As new companies get listed, I will add them to my website.

17. Make your own deal

Make your own deal and post it on all free advertisements, send it to friends, family and colleagues. Just be sure to ask them where they saw the deal posted so that you know which advertisement works better for you so that you know which ones to use next year.

18. Online Directories

Online directories are like Yellow Pages, but online. There are some that are specifically listings for cottages and some that list businesses. Do a search for "online directory" or "cottage listings" and add the city or lake where your cottage is located. Example: "online directory lac simon".

19. Promotional Items

Promotional items are a great way for you to get exposure. Get t-shirts, baseball caps, towels with your logo and cottage website or information added to them. Give them to your friends, family, wear them yourself and also give them as prizes for special events like Tulip Festival or golf tournaments going on in your town and radio stations. Vistaprint offers great deals. A great tool is a car door magnet you put on the outside of your car. People see it everywhere you go every day.

20. Yellow Pages

The Yellow Pages has a book and online directory. They are 2 separate businesses and they both charge a fee, but the book is hardly used anymore unless you're in a small town with not a lot of internet access. I am not a fan of the Yellow Pages for property rentals, but here's the link to get details on size of ads and pricing www.yellowpages.ca.

21. Magazines

There are specific magazines for cottage owners like *Cottage Life, Canadian Homes and Cottages Magazine* and *Cottage Magazine* which has lots of good stuff on how to rent, opening and closing your cottage for the season, recipes, and so much more. There are also ones for travellers. This would be a good place to advertise. You could see about writing an article for them and in return have them advertise your cottage details.

22. Partnerships

Golf courses have events and regular players that may not want to drive back. Ask if you can leave your brochures with them and if they would be willing to post your details on their site, and in return for every rental that comes from them, they will get a finder's fee.

23. Cottage Online Rental Directories

Cottage rental websites are online directories that will advertise your cottage details on their website to people looking to rent cottages. You enter all the details, including your pictures, and they add it to their site. I got many rentals this way and the cost was very reasonable.

Here's a list of rental websites that I like best, but if you search online, you're sure to find more.

> www.cottagesincanada.com
> www.cottagelink.com
> www.rentcottage.com
> www.cottagesquebec.com
> www.onlinecottagerental.com
> www.cottageportal.com

www.atthecottage.com
www.ottawa.kijiji.ca
www.cottagesontheweb.com

24. Business Referrals

There may be businesses around your cottage. Ask them if you can put up posters or business cards on their wall. You could also say for every rental that comes from their link or someone who brings in the ad, you will give them a finder's fee or you could also say you will add their company name to the brochure and website of your cottage (trade for trade).

25. Outdoor Advertising

There is also making an 8 ½" X 11" size flyer or poster and putting them up on outdoor posts throughout your city. Include information like where it's located, how many bedrooms, waterfront or swimming access, and include the price. You don't want to waste your time with people who can't afford your cottage. Before you hang your flyer, check with your city first before you hang posters as some of them do not allow it and will give you a fine if you get caught. Also, bench advertising or bulletin boards get noticed, but they tend to be a bit more expensive. If you plan to use this type of advertising, then I suggest you contact an advertising agency because the prices vary by city.

26. Networking

Networking is an event you go to and introduce yourself and your business. It's not usually the place you go to get sales, but it does happen. What these events are for is to start to meet business people like yourself looking to make connections and help spread the word about your business and find services you may need like a web designer or bookkeeper.

Check online for a networking event in your area. There are many of them around and some don't always stay around.

Contact the Chamber of Commerce, Entrepreneurship Centre or Small Business Associations located near you. I will also post events on my website when companies advise me of events going on.

Property Manager or Rental Agency

When I first started renting my cottage, I was all excited. I was bringing in income, but the emails and telephone calls were getting a bit much. I had a least 10 emails a day asking questions, not necessarily rentals. I was also working a full-time job. Then when I did get renters, I had to make time to meet renters and hand them the keys. Once rental was completed, I had to go up to see if the cottage was clean and nothing broken. This takes a lot of time. So, if you have the time, great, but if not, consider hiring someone. If you don't have time to show the cottage or would rather not drive the distance to the cottage, hire a property manager. You can find listing of cottage property rental agents online in the city your cottage is located.

Do a search under "cottage property rental agent" or "cottage property manager".

For Ontario, I found Ontario Cottage Rentals:

www.ontariocottagerentals.com/rental-management.php

As for Quebec, I wasn't able to find links to property managers in Quebec, but I got feedback from other cottage owners and they said that people in Quebec usually hire a handyman or someone in the town to take care of the property.

Building Your Website

This section will cover what details you should include on your website, where to build a website for free and information on where to get training to build your very own website.

Take note, this is not a book on how to build your website, but rather information.

Do I need a Website?

As the saying goes, if you build it, they will come. You don't need a website, but if you want people to find you, you will need to let people know where you are. If you don't want to build your own website, you can simply add your information to a cottage rental directory for a fee. However, if you want more control of what's on your site and not to mention, save money, it's better to have your own website.

What Should I Have On My Website?

To make a good website visible I have created a mind map on the next page and identified each item that should be on your website:

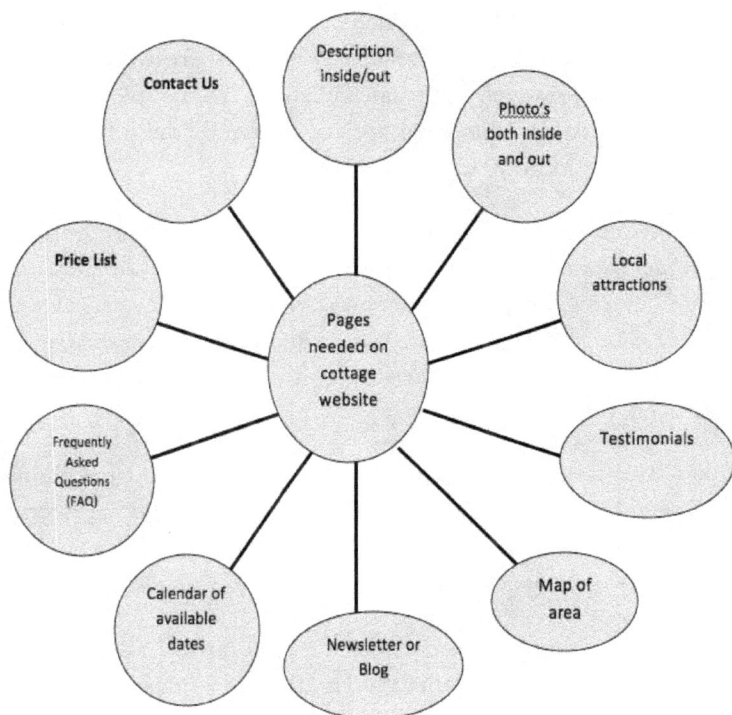

Here's a bit more detail about each of the items shown in the mind map.

Photos – attach photos to the home page as well as a separate pages for all photos of the cottage, lake/river and activities to show how much fun or relaxing it is.

Description – use the info you developed in the section describing my cottage.

Contact Us – Add your telephone and email information for people to get in touch with you to book rentals or ask more details.

Price List – include in your price list one for weekly, weekend, daily and holidays and/or long weekends.

Calendar – you should have a calendar to show the dates you have available so you're not getting calls for dates already booked. You could, however, leave dates blank so that people are forced to call you to see what dates are available and your job will be to get to them to book for another date.

FAQ - Frequently Asked Questions includes a list of questions that renters often ask before they rent, such as location of lake, number of rooms, how many neighbours, how close to water, etc. I have created a list of types of questions I was asked and posted them on my website for you to use to develop your own answers for your FAQ page.

Maps – This is a link on Google maps that you can add and should so people can see where your cottage is located and the river (if available). It's also a place to add the link to the cottage. Go to www.googlemaps.ca to link your cottage to Google.

Newsletter – this is not needed, but it's a good way to draw people to you so you can get more renters because you'll be contacted regularly and you will be the first they contact. Newsletters or blogs have things like recipes, ways to have fun in the rain while on vacation.

Local attractions - list the places close by like artist shows, car shows, sports tournaments like golf and tennis, and wine and cheese tasting events.

Testimonials - Once a renter has rented ask them for feedback or referrals, then ask if they mind if you use their testimonials on your marketing material.

Here's an example of my cottage website
www.tinalalonde.webs.com

When preparing your information, take into consideration Needs versus Nice to Have. Needs being the description of the cottage price list and how people can get a hold of you are very important, but Nice to Have would be something like recipes, or how to fix a bug bite. They are nice to have but not a priority when developing your website. You can add them later, maybe as a blog, but for now, you should focus on the list you provided in Chapter 7 Describing the Cottage.

How Do I Build My Own Website?

To build a website is a bit more work and we will not be covering it in this book. There are many books you can buy that will teach you how to design your own. If you're like me and you're a visual learner, you should take training. You will need a website domain, hosting company, internet site. If you are not familiar with websites and how they work, I suggest you take some training.

Where Can I Get Training to Help Build My Website?

For online training, I recommend you take this online course from *WordPress Academy*. They take you step by step and answer all your questions on domain registration, hosting and what's a website. They offer hosting for your site as well as other suggested hosting companies, and they will show you how to promote your website. Their website is www.wpacademy.tv. If you missed a class, not to worry, they videotaped it for you to download and they have personal coaching sessions to help you fix your website. The training also included 90 days free hosting for my website and a backup buddy which would have cost me $125. These 2 things alone, I saved $150. The main reason I signed up with them was they offered a free course overview on how to build my website in about an hour and I was sold after that.

NOTE: If you sign up for any of the courses they offer through my website www.howtorentmycottage.ca, I will pay you 50% of the commission of what they paid me to have you sign up. I want to help you save as much money as you can.

If you prefer classes, local city school boards website, or college, or small business centre or even online classifieds like www.kijiji.com. My city is Ottawa and my school board is Ottawa Carleton District School Board and their website is www.ocdsb.ca and there's also the local college Algonquin or the French one Cité Collégial. Your local library offers workshops, usually free. There is also Invest Ottawa that have in-class courses that very from 1 day to 8 weeks. The courses are listed usually under Small Business or Computers. I would suggest you call them instead of email as you get a quicker response.

How to Build a Website for Free in 1 Hour

When I started renting my cottage I didn't have a lot of extra money, so I took the chance and created a free website with www.webs.com. It's a great tool, but the only problem is they put advertising on my website. So, people were confused when they would go to my site because there on the front page was a beautiful 5-star cottage, but it wasn't mine. However, it allowed me to show my cottage, describe it in detail and get people to email or call me to book rentals.

It was a good idea at the time and I recommend using a free site if you're on a tight budget, but when you can, I would suggest you use a hosting company with no ads. Here are a few web hosting companies that you can use to build a simple site that has no ads.

The price ranges from $4 to $20 a month:

> www.webs.com
> www.weebly.com
> www.wix.com

Chapter 9
Is it Rental Income or a Business?

Are you making rental income or running a business? Here's how to know the difference and the advantages and disadvantages to each.

Rental Income

Rental income is income earned from renting property that you own or have use of and you charge a fee for it. Revenue Canada's website says as follows:

> "Rental income is income you earn from renting property that you own or have use of. You can own property by yourself or with someone else. Rental income includes income from renting a house, apartments, rooms, space in an office building, or other real or movable property. To determine whether your rental income is from property or from business, consider the number and kinds of services you provide for your tenants. In most cases, you are earning income from property if you rent space and provide basic services only. Basic services include heat, light, parking, and laundry facilities."

Business Income

If you provide additional services to renters, such as cleaning, security, and meals, you may be carrying on a business. Canada Revenue Agency (CRA) defines business income as the more services you provide, the greater the chance that your rental operation is a business.

For more information about how to determine if your rental income is income from property or income from business, go to the Canada Revenue Agency website at www.cra-arc.gc.ca/tx/bsnss/tpcs/rntl/rntlbs-eng.html.

Do I Have to Declare the Income?

Canada Revenue Agency (CRA) states that all income gained must be declared. If CRA determines that you have not declared income, they can go back through all your taxes for up to 10 years and charge you interest on the amount you did not declare and you will need to pay it back!

When you rent out your cottage, you will make money and you will also be able to write off expenses. However, with the money you make, you will also need to declare it with Canada Revenue Agency (CRA). Before you can complete your taxes, you will need to know which way to declare that income. Is it rental income or business income and what's the difference? You can deduct any reasonable expenses you incur to earn rental income. The two basic types of expenses are:

- current expenses
- capital expenses

For more details, please refer to T4036 - Rental Income at www.cra-arc.gc.ca/E/pub/tg/t4036/t4036-e.html#P221_15825

Running the Cottage as a Business

Now that you know you're a business, you need to define what type of business structure you will use. There are 4 types of business structures: Sole Proprietorship, Partnership, Incorporation and Cooperation. In this book, we only cover what's involved running your cottage as a sole proprietor or a partnership. For information on Incorporating or Cooperation, go to Canada Business Network website (formerly Industry Canada) under the topics "Starting your Business and Corporation, Partnership, or Sole Proprietorship" at www.canadabusiness.ca/eng/page/2853.

Here are the definitions

- **Sole Proprietor:** you own the cottage under your personal name.
- **Partnership**: you own the property with another and you cannot do anything unless your partner agrees.
- **Cooperation**: a business that is owned by an association of members.
- **Incorporated**: will protect your personal belongings if you ever get sued. A legal entity that is separate from the owners and shareholders. As a shareholder of a corporation, you will not be personally liable for the debts, obligations or acts of the corporation.

Sole Proprietor

Sole Proprietors has many advantages, but also many disadvantages such as:

- You are fully responsible for all debts for the cottage.
- The profits would be yours alone to keep.
- With you being the sole owner, a creditor or renter can make a claim against your personal or business assets to pay off any debt that is owed to them.
- Taxes may be lowered if your business is not doing so well.
- Income you make would be taxable and added to your current rate, which may put you in a higher tax bracket.
- You work alone.

Partnership

In a Partnership, you would share in the profits and paying the debt for the cottage. If you decide on a partnership, you should draw up a legal document and have a witness or preferably a lawyer sign it so that if the partnership is not working, how you will proceed with dissolving the partnership or buying the partner out. There are similar advantages and disadvantages to Sole Proprietor with Partnership, such as:

- You share in day-to-day operations of the cottage business.
- You share the profits and losses.
- You can both be legally sued and have your assets seized as you are not incorporated.
- If you are losing money with the cottage, you and your partner can declare this on your income tax returns.
- You have someone to work with and bounce ideas off.

What Do I Need to Run My Cottage as a Business?

When running a business, there are certain things you need to make your business legal and ensure you are making a profit such as:

- Registering your business name
- Business number
- Tracking sales
- Writing off expenses
- Charging taxes
- Separate bank account

Business Name - Do I need to register my cottage business name?

Service Ontario says you are legally required to register your business name if you are not operating under your personal name, i.e. first and last name. You will need to register the name under which you are operating as, for example: "Tina's Cozy Cottage" would need to be registered as a business name because it's not a person's name. If you are conducting business i.e. writing contracts from your home, that is the province you need to register the business under and not where the cottage is situated. Consider the cottage as a product you are selling, but where you conduct your business is in your home.

I have provided the links and contact information for Service Ontario and Revenue Quebec on the next page so that you can contact them directly with any questions you may have.

Ontario Residents

For Ontario residents who run their business out of their home office, you will register through Service Ontario in the following 3 ways:

Online: www.ServiceOntario.ca

Mail: Service Ontario
        P.O. Box 1028 STN B,
        Toronto ON M5T 3H3

Call Toll-Free in Ontario: 1-800-565-1921
or 1-888-745-8888

NOTE: For Service Ontario, there is a fee of $60.00 to register your business name

Quebec Residents

For Quebec residents who run their business out of their home, you will register through Revenue Quebec in the following 3 ways:

Online: www.revenuquebec.ca

Mail: Direction principale des relations
avec la clientèle des entreprises
Revenu Québec
3800, rue de Marly
Québec (Québec) G1X 4A5

Call toll free: 1 800 567-4692 or 514 873-4692

Registering a business number – Do I need a number?

A business number is a way for the government to identify your business dealings with the federal and provincial governments. You will only need a business number if your cottage is a business and not a rental property, and offers services, you charge HST taxes (Ontario) or QST and GST (Quebec), or your you will have revenues that exceed $30,000 yearly as well.

Canada Revenue Agency's website as of May 2012 quotes the following:

> "You (resident or non-resident) provide taxable, including zero-rated goods or services in Canada in the course of carrying on business in Canada on a regular or continuing basis and your revenues exceed $30,000 ($50,000 for public service bodies) in a single calendar quarter or in four consecutive calendar quarters" (Canada Revenue Agency. Web. Retrieved from www.cra-arc.gc.ca/tx/bsnss/tpcs/bn-ne/ndn/gst-tps/menu-eng.html).

Tracking Sales and Expenses

It's great when money is coming in from rentals, but you need to know if you're making money with all the extra expenses you are paying to upkeep and renovate the cottage. You will need to keep track of all your sales and expenses with a Sales and Expense Report.

Sales Report

A Sales Report (also known as Accounts Receivable) will be needed to keep track of all the rentals and amounts they paid. A Sales Report should have the following details:

- name of your cottage
- the owner
- the title of the report
- the year
- dates of rentals
- name of renters
- amount paid
- discounts or coupon amounts
- method of payment

Not only is a Sales Report necessary for taxes, it's a good way to see when are your best months for rentals. As well, when it's time to rent the following year, you already have a built list of renters whom you can contact.

Here's an example of a sales report from my cottage.

Tina's Cozy Cottage

Sales Report 2011

Rental Dates	Name of Renter	Amount Paid	Discounts/ Coupon Amount	Method of Payment (cash, cheque, Visa)
June 1 to 3	Tina Lalonde	$300.00	n/a	Cheque
June 18 to 22	John Smith	$150.00	$200.00	Cash
TOTAL		$450.00		

What Are My Expenses?

Expenses are the things that happen on a monthly basis that you must take into consideration when renting. They include:

- mortgage, utilities (electricity, gas, hot water tank rental)
- maintenance (grass cutting, the dock, snow removal, wood cord, road repair, propane tank for BBQ)
- contractors for cleaning and renovations
- property taxes

You will also need to calculate on top of the daily expenses things like advertising fees if you place ads, which I **STRONGLY** recommend you do. Otherwise, how will people know your cottage exists? You may also have a website.

When you start renting, you will need to add the costs of the increase in utilities, wood and propane into your rental. It will all depend on how often you rent, what type of utilities you have i.e.

electric baseboards versus wood stove, and having an oven versus using the BBQ, and cleaning supplies and equipment such as a vacuum. Check with the utility company that you are using to see what last year's estimate was based on a full month of use.

Expenses - 40 Things And People You Can Write Off!

The best part about having a cottage rental business is being able to write off expenses for it. Now, before you start thinking of taking a vacation down south and writing if off as an expense, you need to know the rules as to what you can write off.

List of Expenses

Canada Revenue Agency (CRA) has provided a list of what you can write off as a business expense and they are listed below. If the item is not listed, contact CRA to make sure you can deduct it.

- Advertising (newspapers, magazines)
- Website hosting, domain registration, Internet Service Provider
- Allowance on eligible capital property
- Bad debts (bounced cheques)
- Bank fees, credit card fees & interest
- Books, magazines
- Business registration fees
- Business start-up costs
- Business-use-of-home expenses
- Capital cost allowance
- Charities
- Community fees (maintenance of surrounding property around the lake and our roads)
- Computer hardware/software
- Current or capital expenses
- Delivery, freight, and express

- Utilities (heat, gas, hydro)
- Fees, licenses, dues, memberships, and subscriptions
- Gifts
- GST/HST you incur on these expenses
- Home office
- Insurance
- Interest paid on line of credit or mortgage
- Legal, accounting, bookkeeper and other professional fees
- Licenses and permits
- Maintenance and repairs
- Management and administration fees
- Meals and entertainment
- Medical
- Motor vehicle expenses
- Office supplies
- Prepaid expenses
- Property taxes
- Rent
- Salaries, wages, and benefits (Family, yes you can write them off! Ha Ha…OK, maybe not, but you can deduct them from your expenses, if you have them working for you, you can deduct the wages you pay them.)
- Supplies (cleaning, dishes, linens)
- Telephone/cellular (long distance and answering machine)
- Tools and equipment (hammer, shovel)
- Training to upgrading skills (seminars, workshops)
- Travel (meals, lodging, train, plane)

Expense Report

An Expense Report (also known as Accounts Payable) will be needed to keep track of all the expenses you paid during the year to give to a tax expert or if you're doing your own taxes, which you are NUTS to do. You will add all your receipts to this report. It will provide you with an itemized list and you will be able to add the amounts quickly to your tax returns.

Not only that, but it will also help you to see where you are spending more money and if you need to raise your rental rates. An expense report should have the following details:

- date
- unique item number
- amount
- monthly expense column for items such as advertising, bank fees, internet, car maintenance

Here's an example of an Expense Report:

Tina's Cozy Cottage

Expense Report 2011

Date	Item #	Meals/	Car expense	Insurance	Miscellaneous	Description
2011-06-01	1		300			Car tires
2011-06-03	2				560	Property taxes
Total			**300**		**560**	

NOTE: I suggest you do your Expense Reports at the end of each month, compile all the receipts and add them to the expense report. This will ensure you remember what expenses were purchased for the cottage and which were personal and you don't accidently add them. CRA does do an audit and if they feel your business is being dishonest, they may audit you for previous years, too.

Receipts

You will need to keep all the receipts for items you are declaring on your Expense Report and provide a copy with your year-end taxes. Otherwise Canada Revenue Agency may not consider it an expense.

NOTE: when you are adding up your expense receipts and you have five things on a receipt, but only one is for the cottage, you will need to minus the item from the total bill and add the taxes separately for that one item if there are any. For example, you bought cleaning supplies and roast chicken. Unless you're offering to make dinner for the renters, you will need to minus the amount from the receipt and add the actual amount to the Expense Report.

Getting a GST or HST Number

If you are running the cottage like a business where you offer services like cooking and cleaning, Canada Revenue Agency says then the business rules apply in that once you reach $30,000, you need to start charging QST and GST (Quebec) and HST (Ontario) for your rentals. My recommendation is when you are getting close to the $25,000 amount in rentals, then consider getting a business number. Reason being, it's a lot of paperwork for the amount of taxes you might save.

To get a GST or HST number, go to the CRA website at www.cra-arc.gc.ca and look under "Information for Business" and look for "Registering for GST/HST".

Separate Bank Accountant

Do I need to have a separate bank account for cottage rental? The answer is no and yes. It's a good idea to keep your business separate from personal stuff because Canada Revenue Agency can come to you and say, we'd like to see your bank transactions for period of (whatever date they decide). You may not know what expenses were for the cottage and which were personal.

If you open a new account, you don't need to make it complicated, just ask your bank for a separate account. Some banks like President's Choice Financial and ING Direct offer free chequing and savings. Try to find a bank with the least

amount of fees and make sure they have advantages to using them instead of their competition i.e. they give you something for free like PC gives you free groceries.

If you decide not to separate your cottage stuff from your personal, that's OK. Let's just hope you are good at keeping track of your sales and expenses on paper.

Chapter 10
Taxes and Avoiding Them

Grrrrr, there's that word I hate so much. You're taxed when you work, taxes when you buy food, taxed when you go out, taxed for school. However, these taxes do pave the roads to the cottage and maintain them in the winter so that you can drive up. So sometimes, taxes do help. This chapter will cover the thing that most people hate the most…TAXES and what to do with them, and do you in fact need to charge them, the difference between Ontario and Quebec taxes, GST or HST number, filing your taxes, hiring a professional, and the crazy one, doing your own taxes.

Difference between Ontario and Quebec Taxes

From a federal tax perspective, Canada Revenue Agency (CRA) says that the tax implications are the same regardless of the location of the property in Canada. However CRA does not administer Quebec provincial tax.

Quebec:
www.revenuquebec.ca/en/sepf/services/scr_transmission_decl_rev
enu/default.aspx

Ontario:
www.cra-arc.gc.ca/formspubs/t1gnrl/llyrs-eng.html

Income Taxes - Do Your Own. I Dare You!

If you're patient and want to save money, do it yourself. What's the worst thing that happens? You get audited. It's not a big deal. First thing you need to do is get the guide "General Income Tax and Benefit Guide" from the CRA.

You can get it online at www.cra-arc.gc.ca or at your local post office or ask CRA to mail it to you.

Hire a Professional Tax Expert

This section covers the difference I encountered with accountants, bookkeepers and tax preparers and of course, being silly and doing it myself.

Accountant, bookkeeper or tax preparer? I all can say is HIRE either one because they know the tax laws and the difference between a rental income and a business. How many people like to do their income tax? I don't know about you, but I don't, which is why I hire a tax expert to do mine. It costs me $100 and is worth every penny, even though the pennies are no longer going to be used anymore! I have listed a few I know of in the Hire a Professional section of the book. They know the forms needed, the lingo that Canada Revenue speaks, and what are the rules as to what can be deducted.

I hired a bookkeeper the 1st year, and accountant the 2nd year because I got reassessed. The only difference is the price. I paid a bookkeeper $35 which was good, but he didn't know all the tax laws on what I can write off, so I got reassessed. Next was $475 for three tax reports they completed. I had three of them because I had two home-based businesses and my personal taxes.

The last and the one I use is a tax preparer who actually works for Revenue Canada, costs me $80 and is worth every penny!

Questions to ask when looking to hire:

- Do they work in the accounting field? If so, where like accounting office, Canada Revenue Agency, or their own business?
- Do they do taxes for Ontario and Quebec (depending on which you need they are different)?

- What papers, receipts do they need?
- How much do they charge?
- What are their hours to meet renters?
- Are they willing to come to your house? If not, be sure to find out where they live so that you're not driving an hour out of town. It's not always worth the gas.

Saving money when using a professional

On the next page are a few tips to save you money with your professional service provider:

- Keep your receipts in order by grouping into categories and write on them what they're for
- Add the amounts to a spreadsheet called Expenses and Sales
- Make a copy to give them
- Scan the receipts and send them by email to get started right away
- Have them submit your taxes online to Canada Revenue Agency

The only difference I found to using an accountant, bookkeeper and tax preparer is the price and if you do all the work, why would you be willing to pay $200 to have your taxes done.

How to find a professional tax person?

Most people who are professional tax people usually have a website or are listed in the Yellow Pages. I would ask your friends and family first, or attend a business networking event to meet someone who does income taxes. Another way I found one was I posted a want ad on the internet that I was looking for someone to do my taxes for my small business. I explained what type of business. I got quite a few replies. Be sure they are legitimate. They may only do this part time, and that's OK, after all, you might be renting your cottage part-time. Ask where they work and do they have business card. You can also ask if they would be willing to get references from past clients.

Filing Your Business Taxes

This section will cover what you need from your rental business to complete for tax forms, where to find the tax guide and video links to instructions on how to complete your taxes, and how to do it online. I am not going to show you how to do your taxes because taxes are different for everyone.

Consequences to Not Declaring Your Income

What are the consequences if someone doesn't declare rental income from a rental property? Canada Revenue Agency can go back and audit your taxes and you would have to pay interest on the rental income you received.

Deadline to Submit Your Taxes

Tax deadline is April 30th. Do not miss it! If you do and you owe money, interest will be calculated daily from April 30th until the day they receive your tax report. Ontario and Quebec taxes have different tax forms.

Ontario: www.cra-arc.gc.ca/E/pub/tg/t4036/t4036-10e.pdf.

Quebec: www.revenuquebec.ca/en/sepf/services/l_ta.aspx

NOTE: You should always go directly to the CRA website because their information and rules may change.

Online Tax Programs

Here's a list of places that offer online tax programs for you to use to complete your taxes yourself, if you're brave or crazy enough.

www.drtax.ca/en/UFile.aspx
www.turbotax.intuit.ca (also called Quicktax)
www.genutax.ca

Conclusion

That's everything in a nutshell. I hope this book helps you avoid some of the pitfalls that come with renting your cottage.

Remember one thing, **choose the right renters**. They can be the difference between a pleasant season and an expensive headache.

If you would like help to get new clients quickly, email me at **info@howtorentmycottage.ca**.

If you have additional information that is not in the book or you have experiences that you would like to share, please post comments on my website as I would love to hear about your journey.

Good luck and happy renting!

Tina Lalonde
www.howtorentmycottage.ca

References and Links

Here is the list of websites, books, people and places I've contacted to put this book together.

Abel Pest Control

Canada Revenue Agency (www.cra-arc.gc.ca)

Canadabusiness.ca

Canadian Cottage Insurance

Cottageblogger.com

Cottageliferentals.com

Cottagelink.com

Cottagemania.ca

Cottagetips.com

Ehow.com

Industry Canada

Insurance Bureau of Canada (**www.ibc.ca**)

Insuranceincanada.com

Landlord and Tenant Act

  Ontario - www.ltb.gov.on.ca

  Quebec - www.cmhc-schl.gc.ca

Evelyn Jacks. 3 edition (Nov 29 2006). Make Sure It's Deductible McGraw-Hill

Ontario Cottage Rentals

Municipal Government of Ontario (www.ontario.ca)

Ontariorealestatesource.com

Quebec municipal (**www.quebecmunicipal.qc.ca**)

Rozon Insurance Brokers

Service Canada (www.servicecanada.gc.ca)

Douglas Hunter. 1st Edition (May 6 2006) The Cottage Ownership Guide. Cottage Life Books

Thecompletelandlord.com

Webs.com

Weebly.com

Wordtemplatesonline.com

Health Canada (www.hc-sc.gc.ca/hl-vs/iyh-vsv/environ/wood-bois-eng.php)
eHow (www.ehow.com/how-does_4695252_carbon-dioxide-poisoning-kill-human_.html#ixzz26B3BzA00)

Canadian Centre for Occupational Health and Safety - www.ccohs.ca/oshanswers/chemicals/chem_profiles/carbon_dioxide/health_cd.html

Images - office.microsoft.com

Ontario Ministry of Natural Resources (www.mnr.gov.on.ca/en/Business/LetsFish/2ColumnSubPage/STEL02_164832.html)

Resources naturelles et faune du Quebec – (www.mrnf.gouv.qc.ca/english/publications/online/wildlife/fishing-regulations/regles-generales/fishing-licence.asp)

About the Author

Tina Lalonde is a marketing coach, a teacher and an entrepreneur who has owned 4 successful businesses, one of them being a cottage rental as well as writes instructional guides for private and government departments. She has a post grad in Marketing Management. She lives in Ontario where she spends her time mentoring new entrepreneurs on ways to help them grow their businesses, as well as teaches workshops with the Ottawa Carleton District School Board. She loves to cook creative meals – OK that's a lie – she likes to eat and can't cook. You can't be good at everything.

Email: tina@howtorentmycottage.ca

Website: www.howtorentmycottage.ca

Tel: (613) 324-3035

If you build it, they will come.

Teddy Roosevelt